C000026923

To Richard —

9 months in the institution,
how many do you recognise?
with all my love,

Emma
xx

See N° 64!

Jane Asher is a well-known actress and the author of many bestselling books, including *Jane Asher's Party Cakes*, *Jane Asher's Children's Parties*, *Time to Play* (with Dorothy Einon) and, most recently, her first novel *The Longing*. Along with *101 Things I Wish I'd Known Before I Got Married* are published *101 Things I Wish I'd Known Before I Had Children* and *101 Things I Wish I'd Known Before I Moved House*. Jane Asher is married to the artist and author Gerald Scarfe and they have three children.

101 Things
I Wish I'd Known
Before I Got Married

*Thoughts from those who have
been through it themselves*

Edited by Jane Asher

Illustrated by Rowan Barnes-Murphy

MICHAEL JOSEPH
LONDON

MICHAEL JOSEPH LTD

Published by the Penguin Group
Penguin Books Ltd, 27 Wrights Lane, London w8 5tz, England
Penguin Books USA Inc., 375 Hudson Street, New York, New York 10014, USA
Penguin Books Australia Ltd, Ringwood, Victoria, Australia
Penguin Books Canada Ltd, 10 Alcorn Avenue, Toronto, Ontario, Canada m4v 3b2
Penguin Books (NZ) Ltd, 182–190 Wairau Road, Auckland 10, New Zealand

Penguin Books Ltd, Registered Offices: Harmondsworth, Middlesex, England

First published 1996
10 9 8 7 6 5 4 3 2 1

Copyright © Jane Asher, 1996
Illustrations copyright © Rowan Barnes-Murphy, 1996

The moral right of the editor has been asserted

All rights reserved. Without limiting the rights under copyright reserved above, no
part of this publication may be reproduced, stored in or introduced into a retrieval
system, or transmitted, in any form or by any means (electronic, mechanical,
photocopying, recording or otherwise), without the prior written permission of
both the copyright owner and the above publisher of this book

Set in 11/15pt Monotype Baskerville
Designed in QuarkXpress on an Apple Macintosh
Printed and bound in Great Britain by BPC Hazell Books Ltd
a member of the British Printing Company Ltd

A CIP catalogue record for this book is available from the British Library

ISBN 0 7181 3965 8

I am extremely grateful to my editor Louise Haines and my researcher Merle Nygate for their invaluable help and support. Also, of course, I would like to thank the many people who were kind – and brave – enough to let me use their personal views and experiences in the book. There are some who, understandably, wish to remain anonymous, but I would particularly like to mention the following: Jan Goodman, Chris Hale, Adrian Silas, Neil Blane, Christopher Wilson, Dawn Williams, Martin Hendry, Tricia May, Anji Loman Field, Danielle Fluer, Anita Chisholm, Roger Daniels, Valerie Kay, Audrey Oldman, Tika Cope, Martin Fletcher, Denise Moore, David Miller, Sarah Hill, Eric Schneider, Hilary Boys, John Timperley, Margaret Ousby, Shirley Sugarman, Doreen Halper, Susan Ben-Bassett, Mike Emery.

And my grateful thanks to Rowan Barnes-Murphy for his delightful illustrations.

INTRODUCTION

What an extraordinary challenge it is to set out to live with another person. Whether you are contemplating marriage or moving in with your partner for the first time, there is no doubt that, along with the joys of sharing your life with someone you love, there will be problems.

From those who have experienced these problems – and, in most cases, those joys – I have gathered some thoughts, warnings, pieces of advice and hard-won lessons that I hope will be entertaining, and perhaps even useful, to those about to take the plunge. As with so many things in life, a little humour can help a partnership more than almost anything and I hope that, at the very least, this book will make you smile.

As someone who has experienced living with the same person for over twenty-five years, I wish you as much love and happiness as I have found in the midst of the irritations, frustrations and occasional ferocious arguments that are all part of the rich, tangled pattern of sharing your life with another person. *Jane Asher*

1 ... that comfortable shoes are a necessity on your wedding day. Don't be tempted by anything else, however stunning they look. When you get married you spend most of the day standing up, and by the end my feet were killing me. Trainers would be a good idea: brand-new high heels are definitely not.

Woman, married a year

... that saving money has its drawbacks. We were poor young students, and having the wedding reception at home saved a lot of money. The party was great and everyone enjoyed themselves, but we forgot one important thing: we didn't organize anyone to clear up the mess afterwards. We gaily went off without a care in the world for our honeymoon on the Isle of Wight. Two weeks later we returned to a scene of total devastation – rotting wedding cake, glasses still half-filled and overflowing ashtrays.

Woman, married a year

... that a facial two days before the wedding is risky. I was covered in spots on the day.

Woman, married two years

4   ... to have a wedding list in a department store. I couldn't see the need for it, so spent the first three months of married life trying to take things back that we really didn't want when I didn't even know where they had been bought. We married late, and already had most of the china and saucepans we were given, and if we'd had a list we could have included some of the things we really needed, like a fax modem or a fishing rod.

Woman, married six months

5 ... that however long you have lived together before getting married, and however tired or drunk you are, you must make love on your wedding night. Not only that, but you must give it your all, even though you might just feel like lying down and crashing out. It's a very special night, and if you don't, she may never forgive you.

Man, married four years

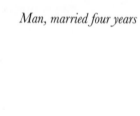

6 ... not to go for the cheapest quote for photography. I let a cousin who was doing a night class take the pictures and I wish I hadn't. When the cake's eaten, the china is broken and the dress has to go back to the hire shop, the photos are all you've got left of the wedding. Go on recommendations, ask to see samples of photographers' work and see if you like their style. And don't forget to order two extra sets of prints – they make wonderful presents for the in-laws.

Woman, married a year

7 ... that you must go to the loo at absolutely the last moment possible before the wedding. It's surprising how long the ceremony lasts, and then you have to sign the register and have the photographs taken, and because you're the centre of attention there's no chance to slip away. Sadly, the strongest memory I have of my wedding day is wondering when I would be able to escape to the bathroom.

Woman, married six months

8 ... to think about whether my dress would fit into the car we would be travelling in. I had a very long train and had to stuff it into a vintage car. Not a good idea.

Woman, married six months

9 ... what my fiancée really wanted. We got married in a register office in front of just a few close friends and then went to a nearby Italian restaurant. It was only years later that my wife told me how hurt she felt by the casual nature of the event. I didn't realize she had wanted the full works, and now I feel sad that we didn't do it that way.

Man, married thirty-five years

10 ... not to pick up the wedding cake at the last minute. We had beautiful lace work on ours that didn't survive the journey, so, on top of everything else, the day before the wedding we had to take the cake back for emergency repairs. If it's fruit, there's absolutely no reason why you can't pick it up a week or so before the day.

Woman, married a year

11   ... to avoid dark green for anyone in the wedding party. This is nothing to do with superstition: it's just that the colour photographs really badly and comes out as brown or black.

Man, married two years

12 ... that when you choose the food for a buf-
fet reception you must make sure that it will
be easy to eat when people are standing up.
Don't go for anything that will fall on to the
guests' clothes or the floor. I'd particularly
recommend avoiding vol-au-vents with a
prawn-cocktail filling: very messy
on blouses and very
squelchy underfoot.

Woman, married
five years

13 ... once you're married there's nothing like the closeness that comes from sharing a private joke in public. You're out with friends and someone uses a word or phrase that means something special to you and your partner. Your eyes meet and for a moment or two you're in a world of your own.

Man, married three years

14   ... that marriage would encourage such creativity. When I met Lisa I was a budding film-maker and she was a student nurse who, amazingly, was prepared to convert to Judaism. Several years and three children later, marriage is not what I expected. Being the next Tarantino is just a daydream, but there's nothing half as much fun and creatively dextrous as holding a new-born in one arm, faxing with the other hand and simultaneously transferring a telephone call from the hall to the study.

Man, married twelve years

15   ... that the statement 'I will have to discuss it with my husband' would magically end a hard sales pitch in a shop or on the doorstep. Persistent salesmen back off immediately. If I'd known that, I would have married much sooner.

Woman, married three years

16 ... that children wouldn't come automatically. I assumed that after a couple of years of blissful togetherness, we would hear the patter of tiny feet. I didn't realize that making babies could involve masked men in white coats injecting goodness knows what up heaven knows where.

Woman, married ten years

17 ... that the wooing – the flowers, the candlelit dinners, the stolen kisses – would stop and that the going down the pub with his mates wouldn't.

Woman, married four years

18 ... that although men may want a woman who is a whore in the bedroom and an angel in the kitchen, what they actually get is someone who's a long time in the bathroom. You may think you know your partner inside out – all those hours talking about dreams and ideas, making love, socializing with other people – but until you've shared a bathroom with her, you don't know anything.

Man, married twelve years

19 ... that I'd never be able to use the bathroom basin. There's always something in it. All I want to do is shave and I can't get near it for a pile of soaking knickers. And we've got a washing machine. The best advice one can give newlyweds who are planning any house renovations is to sacrifice everything for a double sink unit in the bathroom.

Man, married four years

20 ... that a woman who gets ready to go out quickly is worth her weight in gold. It's one of the most wonderful things about my wife.

Man, married
fourteen years

21   ... that women really do take forever to get ready and have to change their outfits five times before they go out. I thought that was a cliché from the cinema and not something we liberated modern couples would have to go through. Not a bit of it. We frequently repeat the same old dialogue.

SHE: Do you like it?

HE: (*Twiddling car keys*) Yes, you look fine.

SHE: What does 'fine' mean? It looks awful. You don't like it, do you?

HE: (*Head in hands*) I do like it. It looks fine ... *great*. I just said.

SHE: You're just saying that. Be honest: you don't like it. I'll try the blue dress.

Repeat until you are late.

Man, married three years

22 ... that we were wrong when we thought we could do it differently. We thought we'd cracked the matter of equality between the sexes, but damn me – who is it who changes the tyre in the pouring rain and climbs up on to the roof to fix the drainpipe?

Man, married six years

23 ... that sustaining a long-term relationship with someone who already has children by a previous partner is difficult. You have to be particularly adult – not easy when you also have needs and emotions.

Woman, married seven years

24 ... that knowing how to have a resolvable argument is the best part of marriage.

Man, married sixteen years

25 ... that you've got to work at a relationship. After we started living together I became really lazy and stopped trying. It lasted another six months. If I'd known that I would lose her, I wouldn't have let it happen.

Unmarried man

26 ... that there are moments of real intimacy in marriage which come at the strangest times. One night I got totally smashed and ate loads of chocolate. My husband helped me undress and held the bowl for me when I threw up. Between retches I said, 'Now I know what true love and devotion are.'

Woman, married three years

27 ... that I would always be expected to stay the same. 'You've changed,' my ex bleated. Well, yes, I'd matured from a gauche girl into an accomplished housewife, gardener, part-time PR executive. He thought he was Peter Pan, but his Wendy grew up.

Divorced woman

28 ... that there are two choices. You can have either a job and money or a husband and kids.

Woman, married sixteen years

29 ... how useless my husband would be with technical appliances. He just can't seem to grasp how the washing machine and dish-washer work. Mind you, he has mastered the video ...

Woman, married eight years

30   ... that parties become less fun after you're married. You know who you're going home with.

Man, married six years

... that his mother would always be there and that no one would ever be good enough for her son.

Woman, married eight years

... that some women can be untidy and some men tidy. When one of you is and the other isn't, life is difficult.

Woman, married seven years

33 ... that you have to be adaptable in all sorts of funny little ways. One of the most serious compromises I still have to strive for with my wife after all these years is walking. She ambles (I say), and I stride (she says). Finding the right balance and speed is very hard work – a bit like marriage itself.

Man, married twelve years

34 ... that we had different body clocks. This certainly makes for some challenging situations. He's up and ready to go to a party at eleven o'clock at night when I'm winding down and ready for bed. And in the morning he's half dead when I'm bouncing around, full of energy. Lunchtime is the best time for us to have any sort of meaningful conversation, so it's just as well that we both work at home.

Woman, living with partner for four years

35 ... that the first time someone referred to me as 'Mrs' I would be totally floored. And that there would be a lot of stammering before I got used to referring to my former boyfriend as 'my husband'.

Woman, married three years

36 ... that courtship seems to involve both parties in being on their best behaviour, while marriage is often an excuse for reverting to type. Those rose-tinted spectacles spontaneously combust when the honeymoon is over.

Woman, married nine years

37 ... that it's stupid to leave an un-
locked honeymoon suitcase in a bedroom.
A liberal scattering of confetti among my
clothes meant that I was shaking it out for
the next two weeks when we were on our
honeymoon. And that the jolly girlfriend
who's loads of fun on a girls' night out is
prone to discuss oral sex in a loud voice after
several glasses of champagne at the wedding reception. Very embarrassing.

Woman, married a year

38 ... how much sport there is on television. I never realized this before I moved in with my boyfriend.

Woman, living with partner for four years

39   ... that a man who doesn't like mushrooms before he gets married will always detect a mushroom in a meal, no matter how cunningly it's disguised.

Woman, married four years

40 ... that once you're married male bosses tend to treat you as mentally and physically challenged. They expect you to become totally stupid and have babies immediately.

Woman, married two years

41 ... that when you and your partner unite against the world, it's as much an expression of love as your love-making.

Man, married four years

42 ... that when people say that two can live as cheaply as one, they're only referring to using the same toothpaste.

Man, married ten years

43 ... that in-laws can create all sorts of problems. If you have any choice, try to choose in-laws who don't speak or who live on a different continent. This cuts down on the 'popping-in' factor, and it also prevents a mother-in-law from tutting at the contents of your fridge.

Woman, married eight years

44 ... how awful the first year would be. I never thought I'd get through it, and I was convinced that I'd made the most terrible mistake. I was twenty-two and he was twenty-four. In the run-up to the wedding Rob – on his own – moved into the flat that we'd both bought and got settled into a routine of bachelor life. Every time I went round there I felt like a guest, but during all the excitement of the engagement and the preparation for the wedding it didn't matter. Afterwards it hit me. I was married but living in a home where I still felt like an intruder on his routine and lifestyle. It took almost a year to adjust, and we had terrific rows about stupid little things like which cupboard to put the coffee in. Eventually we learnt to respect each other's space, but it was hell at the time.

Woman, married four years

45 ... that I would have to learn the hard way – after two divorces. Before the third time I thought I'd better find out what I was doing wrong. Plenty! I reckon there is one thing that you've got to remember. Talk, talk and talk. Talk to your partner about how you feel. Listen to your partner. And be prepared to compromise. Although we do have rows, we're still together.

Woman, married
six years

46 ... that infidelity is a *symptom* of a relationship in difficulty, not a *cause*.

Woman, married fourteen years

47 ... that a tin of baked beans is too much for one person and not enough for two. This was one of the first problems I encountered when I moved in with my boyfriend.

Woman, living with partner for five years

48 ... that during the thrilling days of courting, you can forget to discuss some of the fundamental issues – such as whether your partner wants to have kids. Somehow we neglected to address this matter, which led to major conflicts.

Woman, married nine years

49   ... that when it comes to the wedding, you must make sure that you keep control over events. It's all too easy to be pushed into fulfilling other people's expectations. What started as a small wedding, with only close friends and relatives as guests, snowballed into an all-singing, all-dancing videoed circus, with me strapped and corsetted into an unbelievably uncomfortable dress. My husband reacted badly by getting drunk, and it was not a good start to our marriage.

Woman, married three years

50 ... that discovering your partner has had an affair doesn't have to be the end of the world, though it certainly feels like it at the time. What it *is* is the end of the old relationship. Nothing is the same afterwards. We managed to get through it by talking about why it happened and what was lacking in our marriage. It was incredibly painful, but I think in some ways our marriage is stronger as a result. We both try harder now.

Woman, married seventeen years

51 ... that you needn't worry too much about the ravages of time. I met my husband on a beach. He was lean, dark, with beautiful eyes and long, dark, curly hair. Twenty years later he's still got the eyes, the colouring and hair, but he's trebled his weight and is a long way from the slight youth I met on the beach. I married a Baywatch boy who grew into the Goodyear Blimp.

Woman, married twenty years

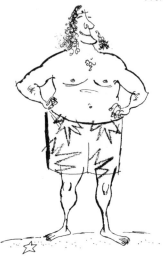

52 ... that my husband would start talking and singing as soon as he woke up in the morning. Some people may consider early-morning chats endearing, but someone saying, 'Talk to me, talk to me. What's your view on the meaning of life?' when you're half asleep is not a great way to start the day.

Woman, married three years

53 ... that my husband is a terrible driver. It wasn't an issue until he was driving me to the hospital to have our first child. I was in the later stages of labour and the baby was bearing down, so I was doubled up, screaming, 'Faster! Faster!' He was creeping along at about twenty miles an hour.

Woman, married three years

54 ... to remake my will. It automatically becomes invalid after you get married.

Man, married thirty years

55 ... that you shouldn't make assumptions about your partner before you get married. My husband assumed that because I worked for an accountant I would be extremely organized and a whiz at managing the household finances. The first time I was overdrawn on my account he realized his mistake ...

Woman, married sixteen years

56 ... how his choice of clothes would change. During our courtship, my husband was always a picture of sartorial elegance. After we got married, over the weekends his true style emerged. The worst was a disgusting old tweed jacket he insisted on wearing despite the fact that the sleeves were three inches too short. It was like going out with Worzel Gummidge – and he totally refused to give it away.

Woman, married twenty-two years

57 ... that being a friendly and sociable type meant that my husband would often invite people back for a meal – frequently without warning ...

Woman, married three years

58 ... that my husband would hate noise so much. We married young and had three boisterous sons in fairly quick succession. I didn't realize what a trial the noise and mess was for him until he insisted on having his breakfast at a separate table.

Woman, divorced three years

59 ... that marriage doesn't need to be romantic to work. Generally, we plod along, go to work, come back, eat dinner, blob out in front of the telly and fall asleep. It's certainly not the stuff of Mills and Boon. Romance – what's that? But when the chips are down, my husband knocks the spots off any man in a Milk Tray commercial. When my mother, youngest son and grandmother were all in hospital at the same time, he was a fortress of support, kindness and humour. So I don't really mind when he snores on the sofa the rest of the time.

*Woman, married
eleven years*

60 ... that I wouldn't mind my husband's faults. His complete ineptitude in the garden is even rather charming. I once actually watched him separate and plant weeds exactly six inches apart.

Woman, married three years

61 ... that the marriage contract would include remembering my husband's family's birthdays and anniversaries. I'm sure I'm the one who gets blamed when the birthday cards don't arrive.

Woman, married four years

62 ... not to hang on to my wedding dress. It hung in the cupboard for six months before being moved to the loft where it went grey. I finally took it to the charity shop two years ago. It would have been much better to sell it soon after the wedding – I would have got some money for it, and someone else could have enjoyed wearing it while it still looked good. You may think you'll cut it down and wear it again but nobody ever does.

Woman, married eight years

63   ... that because my wife retains her single name – and why on earth shouldn't she? – I would frequently be referred to as Mr Her-Surname. It's very disconcerting. Heavens, I hope I'm not losing my identity!

Man, married two years

... that the pleasure of receiving a cup of tea in bed in the morning would never dim. Nor does a warm body to put my feet on. A Teasmaid and a hot-water bottle would not be the same.

Woman, married twenty-two years

65 ... that my husband's interests were broader than I guessed. When I first started going out with him he told me that his passions were classical music and opera. He failed to mention his other interest: horror films. I'm having to get used to emerging from the cinema white-faced and trembling.

Woman, married ten months

66 ... that the most bizarre thing would happen when my husband watches TV. He goes quite deaf and can't hear a thing I'm saying ...

Woman, married three years

67 ... how I would see my wife over the years. I married the most beautiful woman in the world – but I never expected that I would think that half a century later.

Man, married fifty-two years

... that any couple who stay together and are still happy after ten years deserve a medal.

Man, divorced two years

69 ... about the real problem. They say adultery, domestic violence and alcoholism are the most common reasons for marital breakdown. They forgot snoring.

Woman, divorced four years

70 ... that before marrying every couple should be made to take an exam in communication, the organization of domestic roles/tasks, managing a household budget and mutual decision-making. If either partner fails, he or she should have more lessons and resit the exam. If either fails continually, the couple is obviously not meant to marry.

Man, divorced six years

... that when women learn to separate love from sex, there will be more successful marriages.

Man, divorced three years

72

... that in a relationship money is important only if you haven't got it.

Woman, married six years

73 ... that being unemployed brings further punishment when your partner expects you to do the shopping, make the bed, clean the flat and have dinner ready every evening.

Man, married eight years

74 ... that for a couple to hold different polit-ical views can provoke healthy debate, but opposing views about money can start long-standing, bitter rows.

Man, married ten years

75 ... that all marriage contracts should be renewable after ten years.

Man, married twelve years

76 ... that my in-laws would become such friends. I knew a major breakthrough had been made when, after several months of going out with my girlfriend before we got married, her parents stopped referring to me as 'your friend' and discovered that I had a name.

Man, married three years

77 ... that a relationship is like a job. You have to work at it. It might also help if every three months you assessed it and discussed the objectives and necessary adjustments. And if it's not satisfactory, you could apply for a transfer.

Man, living with partner for a year

78 ... how good it is to stay in. You know you're both getting comfortably settled together when you tell lies to your wild and single friends to avoid going to parties.

Man, married eleven years

_79_ ... that the bathroom cabinet would be like the Tardis. It's amazing how much it contains – how many different applications and unguents for all sorts of beauty-making possibilities. Myself, I think she looks all right without them.

Man, married three years

80 ... that she wouldn't manage to wash my clothes with a view to their longevity and current size. Now, you may argue that I could wash them myself, but then I'd miss the fun of complaining.

Man, married ten years

... that if you want to pursue a favourite activity, it's always better to prefix the suggestion with 'Let's ...', as in 'Let's watch *Match of the Day* ...'

Man, married six years

... that there's an interesting mathematical equation in domestic life: two people can fill a dishwasher faster than one person, and they take six times as long to unload it.

Woman, married nine years

83 ... how good it would be. It sounds unbearably sloppy, but when I've had a tough day at work – disappointments and setbacks – and I'm angry with the world, my partner knows what to say and shares my frustration with me.

Man, living with partner six years

... that simple things would annoy her so much. I love using the TV zapper. I can follow two programmes at once, and it's great to know what's on the other side. This irritates the hell out of my wife. For the life of me, I can't think why.

Man, married nine years

85 ... that he'd be too proud to ask for directions when we're in the car. I'm sure it's the testosterone that stops him. We can be driving around for what seems like hours before he agrees to stop the car, admit that we're lost and ask a passer-by.

Woman, married eight years

... that all the fears I had about the enormous lifetime commitment we were making were shared. It's good to realize that I wasn't alone in taking the plunge.

Man, married six years

87 ... that my wife would buy so much food. Before I lived with her I always kept the food in my fridge limited to the amounts I was likely to use. If I ran out of essentials, I went out and bought more. When my wife moved in, she gained a lot of security from having a fridge stuffed with food at all times. We often end up having last-minute dinner parties to clear the fridge out. Big hassle, but quite fun when we have the party.

Man, married two years

88

... about her secret addiction. Forget about her passion for ice cream and chocolate – popcorn is the one she didn't tell me about. Before we got married she kept it under control. OK, there was the odd box or two at the cinema and maybe some for us at home if we were watching a video. But it was only after we were married that it all came out. No matter how much we ate for dinner, by 9 p.m. she was ready for her fix. I quite like popcorn myself, but by the time I'd put on an extra stone something had to be done. We go out for a run now, and by the time we get home the craving has passed.

*Man,
married
two
years*

89 ... about taking criticism. I always believed that if someone loved you, they wouldn't criticize you, and that if they did, they must hate you. When I first met my wife, I was confused. She criticized me but claimed that she loved me. I was very hurt until I confronted her with how I felt. That's when she explained that she wasn't criticizing me, just trying to help. And she did it because she loved me. What a difference that made. Now I don't get angry when she makes comments – and the funny thing is that now she hardly ever says anything that sounds critical.

Man, married three years

90 . . . that my social life would need adjusting. After all, it's hard enough to get round to seeing all the people you know and like when you're single, let alone when you're married. For a long time we felt cut off from our friends and blamed each other. Finally, one weekend we took the plunge and each invited our best friends to dinner at the same time. The evening was not only a great success but led to the other two couples becoming friends as well. This has encouraged us all always to hold our dinner parties jointly.

Man, married two years

91 ... how differently men and women communicate. It ought to be taught at school. For me talk is information, and for her it's interaction. She shows her understanding of another woman's feelings in a directly sympathetic way. I change the subject or paint a less bleak picture to respect an independence. Sometimes we could be talking different languages.

Man, married four years

92   ... that he would be a better cook than I am. I never suspected it, and it has its down side – like when he tastes something I've made and suggests adding perhaps a touch more garlic. But it does mean that we have a lot of fun reading recipe books together and enjoying ourselves in the kitchen.

Woman, married two years

93 ... that bed would be such a problem. I take advantage of my wife on a nightly basis – or so she complains. And I do it even in my deepest sleep. How? By taking up too much of the bedding or infringing her bed space. What am I supposed to do? Cut off my legs?

Man, married three years

94 ... that after years of being single and sleeping in a double bed it would be absolute hell to get used to sleeping in a four-foot-six bed with a six-foot-two man. The greatest investment we made in our marriage was buying a king-size bed. It takes up most of the bedroom, but it saved our relationship.

Woman, married ten years

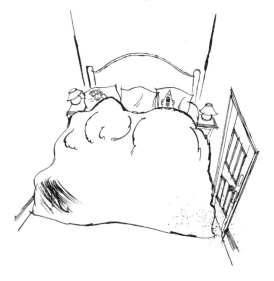

95 ... not to put away his things for him. When I first moved in with my boyfriend he used to take his clothes off at night and leave them on the floor. For quite a while I picked them up and put them away. He must have thought the clothes fairy was living with us. Eventually I got fed up and told him that I assumed that anything left on the floor was rubbish. The first morning of the new regime, as he headed for the door to go to work, I started throwing his clothes out into the street and watched as he rushed around in a panic picking them up. He never left his clothes on the floor again.

Woman, living with partner three years

96 ... how secure I would feel. I remember waking up on the first morning of our honeymoon, pinioned to the bed by my husband's leg and held tight against him as he slept. I remember thanking God for his being there. These days it's usually a mad rush to get the kids up and breakfasted, but I do remember that moment.

Woman, married seven years

97 ... how his sense of humour would help me. Through all the years, the trials and tribulations of life, my husband has always made me laugh. It certainly helps.

Woman, married twenty-six years

98 ... that sex needn't be exhausting to be fun. You may have loads of innovative sex during the early days, but it's rather good when it settles down to a comforting foot-massage in front of the telly.

Man, married thirty-two years

99 ... that it's wonderful if your personalities are similar. There are two sorts of people in the world: those who think everything's their fault and the others who never take the blame. As a New Man with an A-level in guilt, it's tremendously refreshing to have a partner who shares responsibility for the rain, the car breaking down, the keys being lost and the little frustrations of life.

Man, married a year

100

... how important she would make me feel. I like the feeling of being there for her. One time I was at work and I got this frantic phone call. She's terrified of moths and she was stuck in the bedroom with what she described as a 'monster'. I raced across town and got rid of the moth. It wasn't a major danger, but it was nice to be able to do it.

Man, married three years

101 ... how much I would enjoy our late-night chats. Before I was married I never imagined how much fun it would be to go to a party and then come back and talk about everybody.

Man, married two years